Big Bang!

The Tongue-Tickling Tale of a Speck That Became Spectacular

Carolyn Cinami DeCristofano
Illustrated by Michael Carroll

Charlesbridge

The universe is enormous, and it is everything:

everything,
from the tiniest bits of dirt between
your toes to the grandest galaxies;

everything,
from the brightest flashes of light
to the darkest black holes;

everything,
from solid rock
to empty space.

How did our enormous universe begin? What was it like when it started?

These are big questions, and scientists have a big answer:

the **Big Bang.**

An astronomical Big Bang

Changed the
crunched-up
universe, causing
the current cosmos.

Everything we know was once
crunched into a tiny speck.

The universe began in one instant, billions of years ago. Astronomers call this moment the Big Bang.

Try to imagine the universe at that moment. First, forget what you see today. Everything was in a different form. There were no trees, no sky — no Earth. Nothing was alive. There were no planets, no stars, no galaxies.

There was just a single, little, itty-bitty point — kind of like a tiny speck.

The speck was smaller than the tip of your little finger. Smaller than a freckle or a flea. It was even smaller than a freckle on a flea — if fleas could get freckles.

It was the smallest thing that ever was.

The speck may have been tiny, but it sure was stuffed with stuff.
It was incredibly dense.

Imagine packing the speck as if it were a backpack. Try scrunching in
your books and clothes. Now squeeze in your lunch and, while you're at it,
one hundred Mount Everests.

Go ahead, cram it all in together . . . along with a few Earths,
a hundred Suns, and a thousand solar systems.

The speck was even more densely packed than this.

It was also hot — the hottest anything has ever been. Hotter than an oven
or the center of the Sun. Much hotter.

In other words, the early universe was small, crowded,
and hotter than hot.

Then **something happened.**

Dense dust —
and, evidently,
everything else —

Expanded
in a furiously fast frenzy.

The universe . . . sneezed!

Well, sort of.

No one knows why, but the universe suddenly expanded.
In a blip of a moment, it stretched out, like a balloon
being blown up all at once.

The "sneeze" lasted less than a second. But in that time,
the itty-bitty speck became large enough to see.
Now it was bigger than a flea, bigger than the tip of
your little finger, maybe even the size of a basketball.

What a stupendous change! Imagine this
happening to a gum ball. Instantly, the gum ball
would be bigger than the entire universe is today.

This sudden stretch changed the speck.
Right away, the universe became a little less
cramped and a little less raging hot.

Less than a second later, something else happened. Brand-new bits of matter formed, like super-small hailstones. These bits zoomed around, crashing into each other. With every crash, the bits vaporized into bursts of energy.

Meanwhile, the universe kept on expanding, although much more slowly. Moment by moment, as the universe grew, the bits had a little more room to move . . .
      and things got just a little less hot . . .
         and the bits slowed down a little. . .
            until, by the time the universe was three minutes old,
               some of the crashing bits had slowed down just enough to stick together.

               These stuck-together bits were a big deal.
               They became part of the first atoms, and atoms make up lots of things —
               stars, planets, Earth, us. We are here because of the stuck-together
               bits of the young, growing universe.

Good gracious!

The universe
is getting bigger
and **bigger**,

Gaining in girth,
growing genuinely
gigantic!

The universe kept on growing and cooling.
Changes kept happening. Over the next billion
years or so, the first stars, galaxies, and planets formed.

On and on, the expansion continued. Stars, galaxies,
and planets exploded, crashed, and died out. New ones
formed from their scattered remains.

For billions of years, the universe stretched

and

stretched

and

s t r e t c h e d .

And you know what? It is still stretching today.

Hmm . . . How do we know?

A hundred years ago,

we hardly had a hunch.

However, investigations implied

and

justified a jump to new knowledge.

How did we find out about the Big Bang?

In the 1920s, astronomers were studying the light from other galaxies when they discovered something strange. Galaxies are racing away from each other in every direction, moving farther and farther apart.

What could this mysterious motion mean?

Hmm . . . .

Well, if the galaxies in the universe are moving apart, then maybe the universe is expanding like an inflating balloon.

Picture a balloon with dots all over it. The balloon is like empty space. The dots are like galaxies. The dots start out close together. However, as you blow up the balloon, the dots get farther away from each other, just like the galaxies in the expanding universe.

What a kick!

Galaxies are leaving each other,

Mainly moving apart,

not nearer.

If the universe is expanding like a balloon, then the universe grows a little bigger every day. The galaxies will be farther apart tomorrow than they are today.

This means that

yesterday, they were closer together than they are today;
two days ago, they were closer than that;
two years ago, even closer;
two hundred years ago, closer still.

Billions of years ago, all of the stuff of the universe would have been packed together in one crunched-up speck — the speck that started it all.

Today's expanding universe points to a Big Bang beginning long, long ago.

Olden-time observations piqued philosophers'

(Psst...that means prompted people's

penchant for probing

preference for poking into

quintessential

quite long-lived

questions.

questions!)

Curious people in ancient times arranged stones in circles to mark where the Sun, Moon, stars, and planets rose at different times of the year. Stonehenge is one of these circles.

The idea of a Big Bang beginning
came from a whole lot of thinking by
a whole lot of people over a whole lot of time.

Even in prehistoric days, people around the world noticed
the Sun, Moon, and stars moving across the sky. They wondered:

How did the universe begin? What is it made of? How does it work?

They made up stories to explain what they saw.

Eventually, some thinkers started to wonder about the details.
These ancient philosophers sought more answers, starting a
        head-scratching,
            chin-rubbing,
                gadget-making,
                    measurement-taking
                        chain of *hmm*s and *aha*s
                        that has lasted for thousands of years.

Recent researchers
seek scientific solutions
with telescopes
and other tools,

Today, the head scratching continues.

How did the universe begin? The answer, as far as anyone can tell, is the Big Bang. But the Big Bang answer leads to other questions, such as:

What caused the Big Bang?

Why did that speck of an early universe expand?

How did the first stars and galaxies form?

Seeking answers, scientists use powerful new telescopes to investigate parts of the universe that no one has ever seen before.

Sombrero Galaxy

Eagle Nebula

Helix Nebula

Today, powerful telescopes orbit the Earth to help us explore deep-sky objects. These images were taken by the Hubble Space Telescope.

23

Telescopes gather and magnify light from space. Some of this light is the kind we ordinarily see. This includes colors, such as red, green, or blue, or mixtures of colors, which can appear white. All of this is called visible light.

But there's more to light than what we can see. Some light is invisible. We don't see it because our eyes can't respond to it, just as our ears can't pick up the high-pitched tone of a dog whistle.

This invisible light is all around us. It can even ride in sunbeams. For example, ultraviolet (UV) light is a part of ordinary sunshine. When it lands on your skin, it can give you a suntan or even a sunburn.

Some telescopes use cameras to take pictures of the invisible UV light from space. Other telescopes detect X-ray, infrared (IR), and other types of invisible light.

These are radio, infrared, visible light, ultraviolet, and X-ray pictures of the same place in space: the Crab Nebula. They look different because they were taken with telescopes that detect different types of light.

Trying to interpret tales told by unseen ultraviolet light and other waves . . .

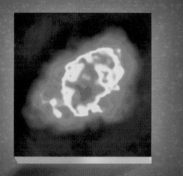

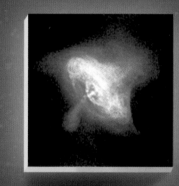

radio   infrared   visible light   ultraviolet   X-ray

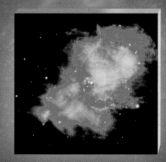

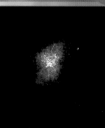

X-,
IR, and microwave rays.

According to the Big Bang theory, when the speck first expanded, it released light energy. The light filled the small but stretching universe. It should still be there, scattered throughout space in a pattern of invisible microwave light.

To test this idea, astronomers used special telescopes to search for the invisible light pattern. They found it — exactly as they had predicted! Evidence like this strengthens the Big Bang theory and tells us a little more about the beginning of the universe.

Invisible microwave light is all around us, secret evidence of the Big Bang. Microwave-detecting telescopes help us "see" this light, revealing the patterns it makes in the sky.

Yet the universe
remains zipped up.

Will it ever
reveal its ways?

Every discovery leads to new questions. Every question leads
to further exploration.

How big is the universe? Does it have an end?

Will the universe always spread out — or could it collapse
in a Big Crunch billions of years from now?

Was the small speck's Big Bang really the beginning of
the universe? Or was there something else before it?

The whole story is still untold. The universe keeps its secrets zipped up.

It hasn't revealed them all,

at least

not

yet.

GLOSSARY

Astronomers Scientists who investigate stars, planets, and other things beyond Earth.

Atom The smallest amount you can have of a basic material, such as the copper in a penny or the calcium in your bones.

Big Bang theory A scientific explanation of how the universe began.

Black hole What is left when an especially big star burns itself out. Light that hits a black hole never leaves it, making the black hole very dark.

Cosmos The universe.

Dense Filled with matter that is packed together very closely.

Energy What it takes to make something happen; for example, what it takes to change something, move it, or heat it up.

Expand To stretch out or grow.

Galaxy A group of billions and billions of stars, surrounded by empty space.

Infrared (IR) light A type of invisible light that has less energy than visible light but more energy than microwave light.

Invisible light Light we cannot see with the unaided eye.

Light A form of energy.

Matter Stuff, substance, or material.

Microwave A type of invisible light with less energy than infrared light but more energy than radio waves.

Radio wave A type of invisible light with less energy than microwave light.

Solar system Our Solar System includes our Sun, everything that moves around it, and the space in between. There are other solar systems in the universe, made of objects moving around other stars.

Star A large, extremely hot ball of glowing gas.

Theory A big idea that explains lots of smaller questions and observations.

Ultraviolet (UV) light A type of invisible light with more energy than visible light but less energy than X-rays.

Universe The complete and total collection of everything that exists.

Visible light Light we can see with the unaided eye.

Wave The motion of energy from one place to another.

X-ray A type of invisible light with more energy than ultraviolet light.

The universe has been around for billions of years.
If you could lay out its entire history on this ruler,

The Big Bang
would be here . . . .

And all of human history would be here, in a skinny splinter
at this end. The splinter would include everything from
the first people's lives to your own.

13.7 billion years ago . . .

Today

To Barry, for bringing me the universe. — C. C. D.

To Caroline, Andrew, and Allie, who always help me experience
the vast and wacky dimensions of the universe! — M. C.

The author also gratefully acknowledges Mrs. Dempsey and her
fifth grade Universe Discussion Group at the Beatrice H. Wood
Elementary School in Plainville, Massachusetts.

Special thanks to R. Hank Donnelly of the Harvard-Smithsonian
Center for Astrophysics.

Credits: Page 23: Helix Nebula: NASA, NOAO, ESA, the Hubble Helix Nebula Team,
M. Meixner (STScI), and T.A. Rector (NRAO), Eagle Nebula: Jeff Hester and Paul Scowen,
Sombrero Galaxy: NASA and the Hubble Heritage Team (STScI/AURA); Page 25: Radio Crab
Nebula: NRAO/AUI/NSF, Infrared Crab Nebula: Keck Observatory, Optical Crab Nebula:
Courtesy of Paul Scowen and Jeff Hester (ASU) and the Mt. Palomar Observatory,
Ultraviolet Crab Nebula: Ultraviolet Imaging Telescope, NASA, STScI, X-ray Crab Nebula:
NASA/CXC/SAO; Pages 26-27: Background courtesy of NASA and the WMAP Science Team;
Page 30: NASA, NOAO, ESA, the Hubble Helix Nebula Team, M. Meixner (STScI),
and T.A. Rector (NRAO); Page 31: NASA and Jeff Hester

Published by Charlesbridge
85 Main Street, Watertown, MA 02472
(617) 926-0329 • www.charlesbridge.com

Library of Congress Cataloging-in-Publication Data
DeCristofano, Carolyn Cinami.
Big bang! : the tongue-tickling tale of a speck that became spectacular /
Carolyn Cinami DeCristofano ; illustrated by Michael Carroll.
    p. cm.
ISBN 1-57091-618-7 (reinforced for library use)
ISBN 1-57091-619-5 (softcover)
1. Big bang theory—Juvenile literature. I. Carroll, Michael, ill. II. Title.
QB991.B54D43 2005
523.1'8—dc22   2004010085

Printed in Korea
(hc)   10 9 8 7 6 5 4 3 2 1
(sc)   10 9 8 7 6 5 4 3 2 1